My Nana A to Z

Fill In The Blank Gift Book

Printed in USA

Published by K. Francklin

Cover Image: Produced by K. Francklin

ISBN-13: 978-1518619335

ISBN-10: 1518619339

I Love My Nana Because…

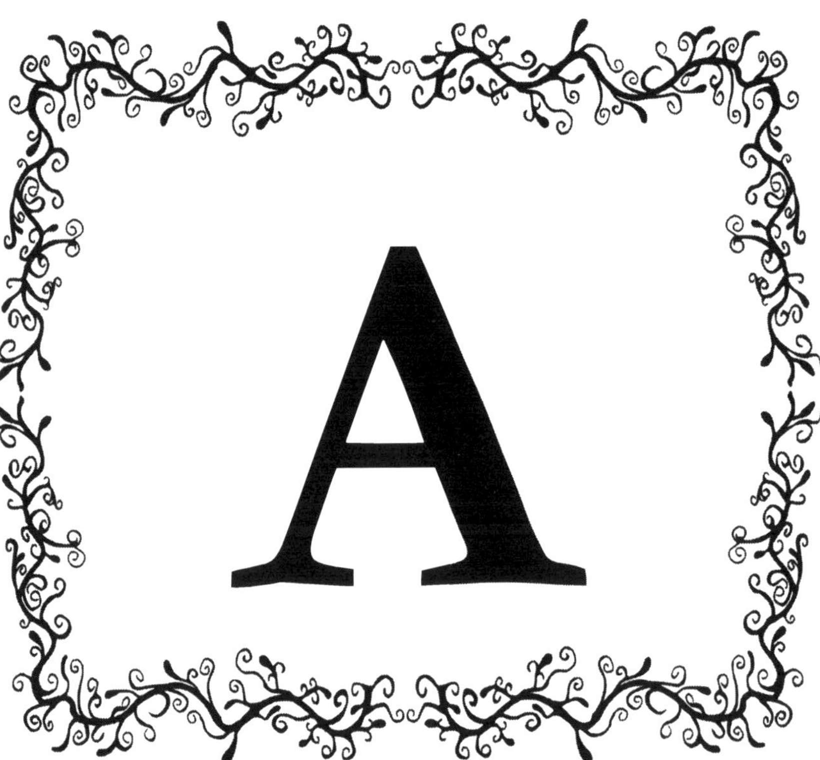
A

My Nana is…

A______________

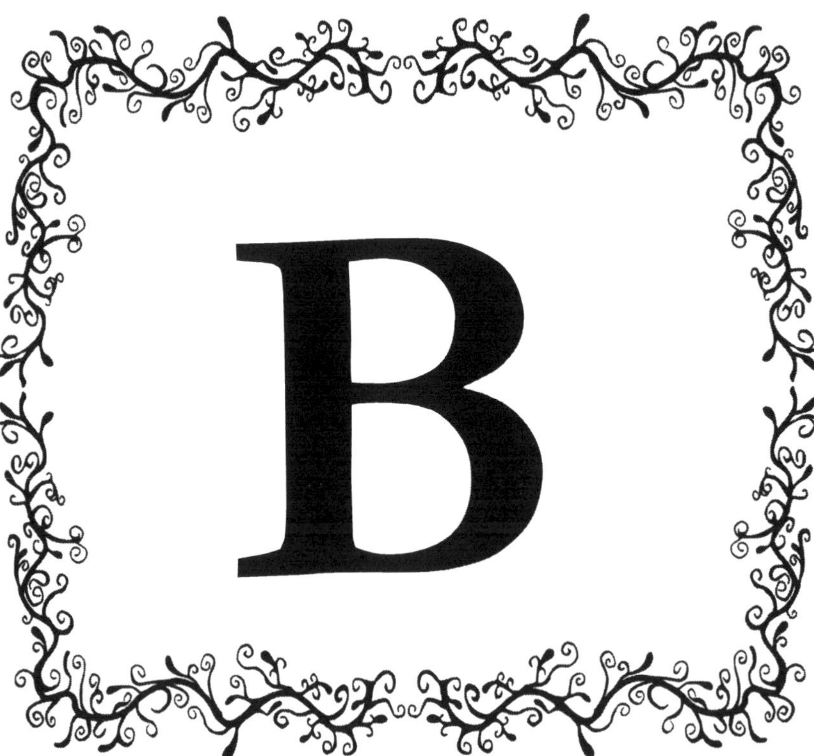
B

My Nana is…

B_______________

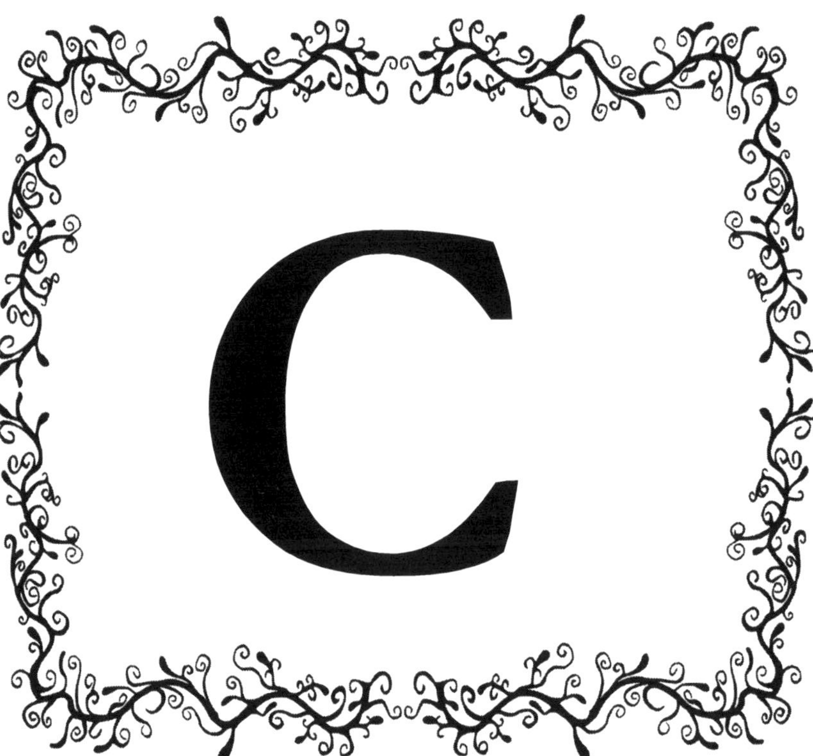
C

My Nana is…

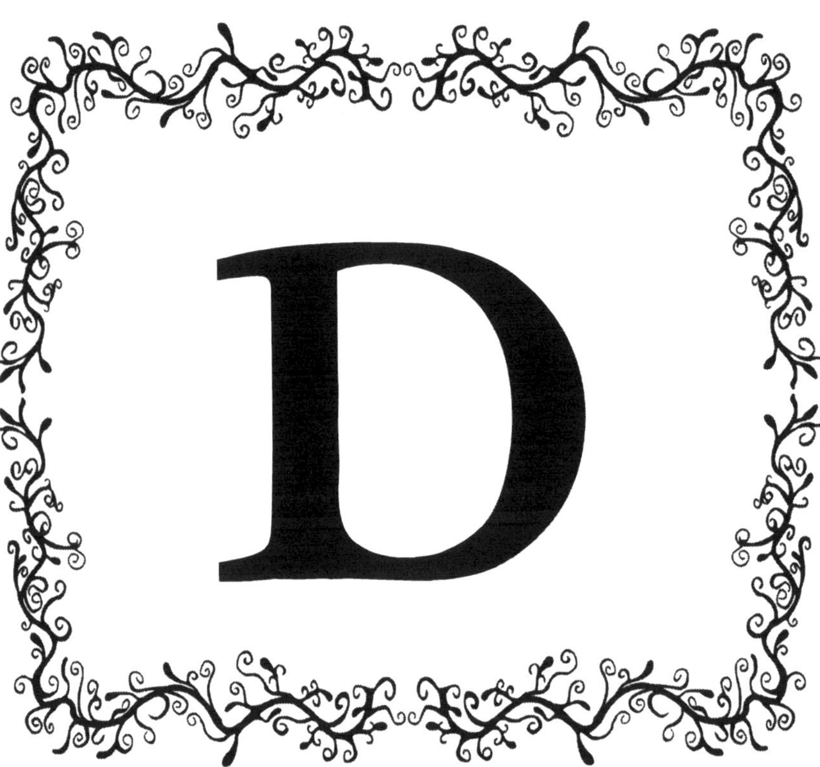
D

My Nana is…

D________

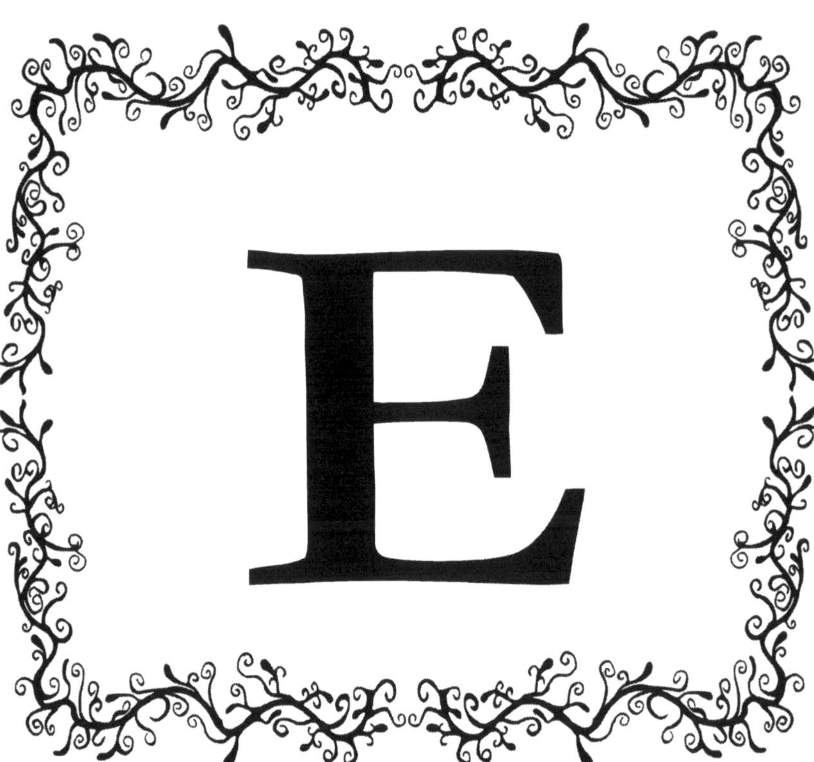
E

My Nana is…

E________

F

My Nana is…

F__________________

G

My Nana is…

G________

H

My Nana is…

H________________

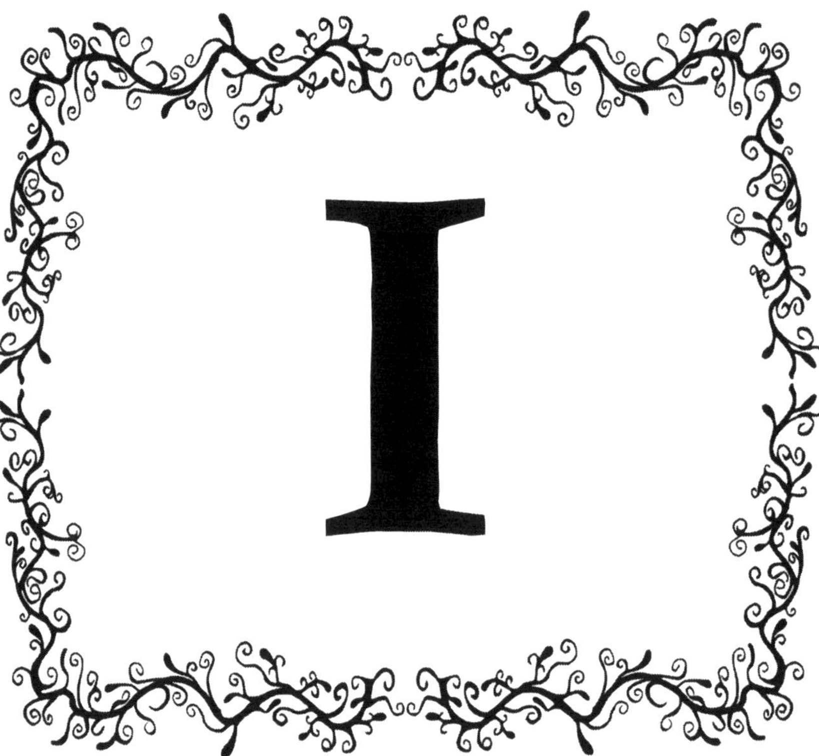
I

My Nana is...

I___________

J

My Nana is…

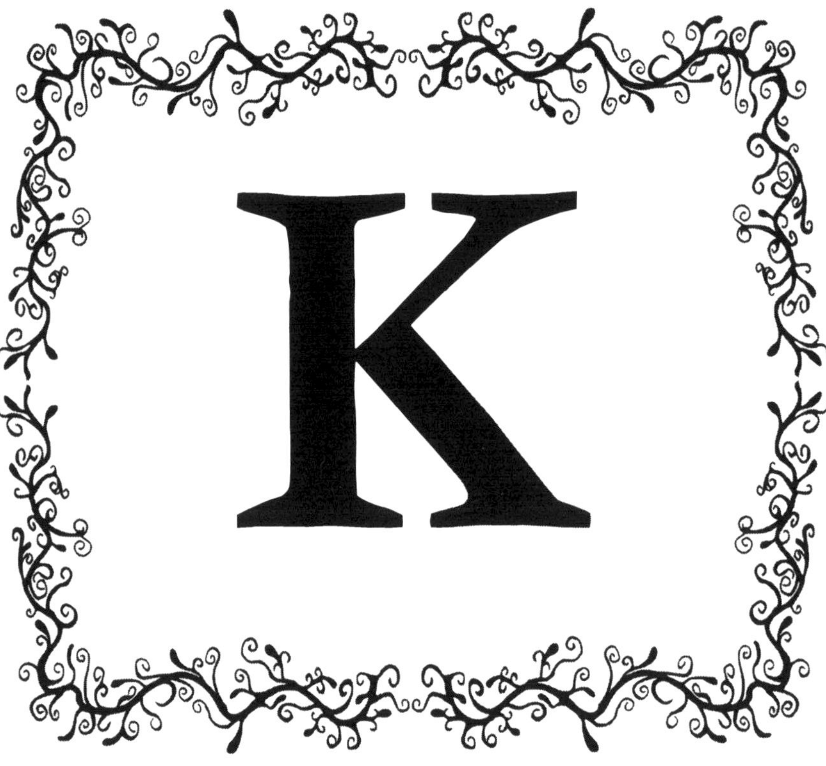
K

My Nana is…

K_______

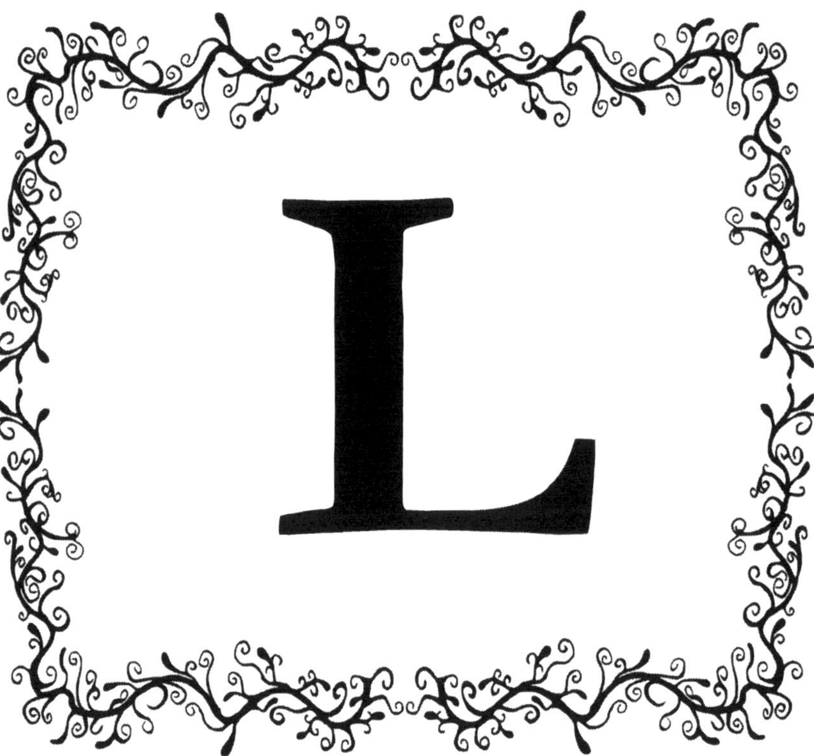
L

My Nana is…

L________________

M

My Nana is…

M________________

N

My Nana is…

N________________

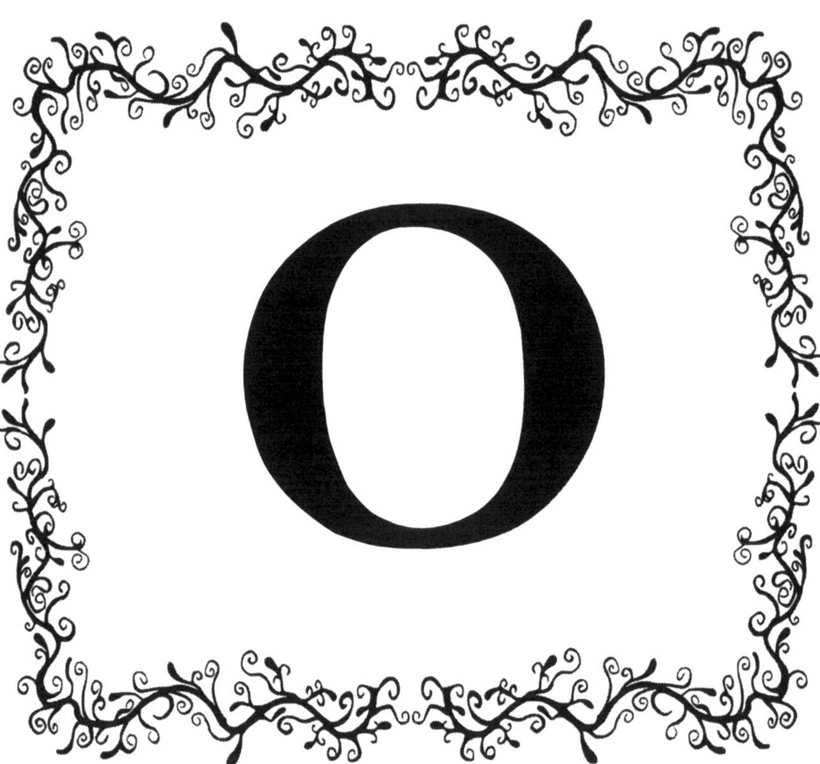
O

My Nana is…

O________________

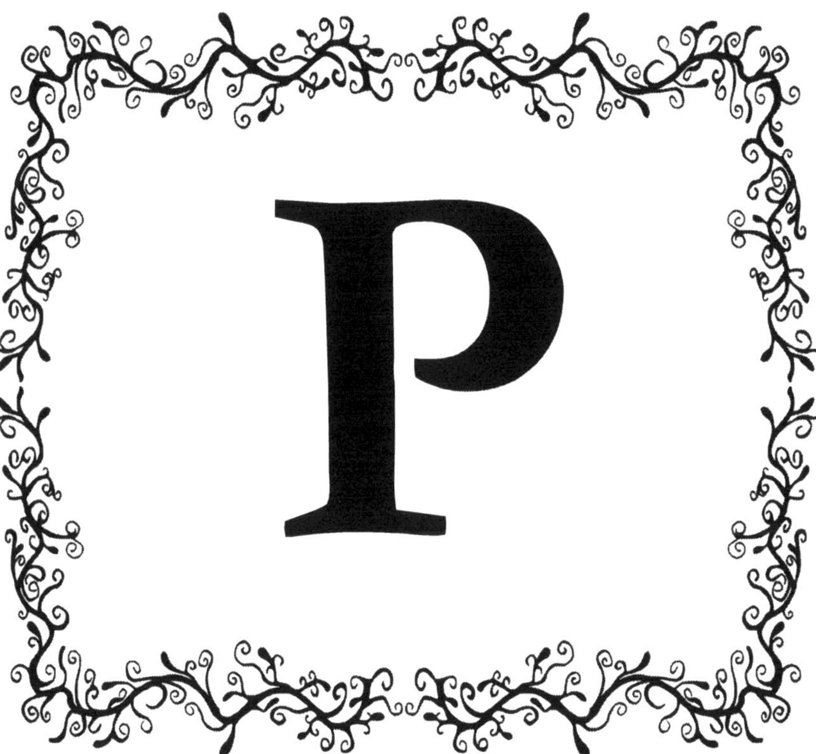
P

My Nana is…

P__________________

Q

My Nana is…

Q_______________

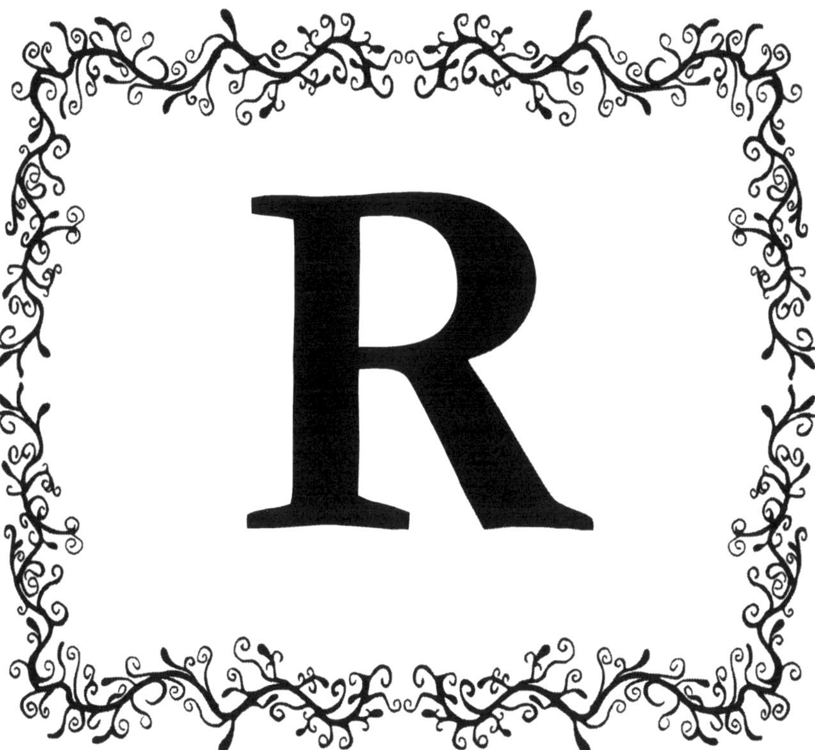
R

My Nana is…

R________________

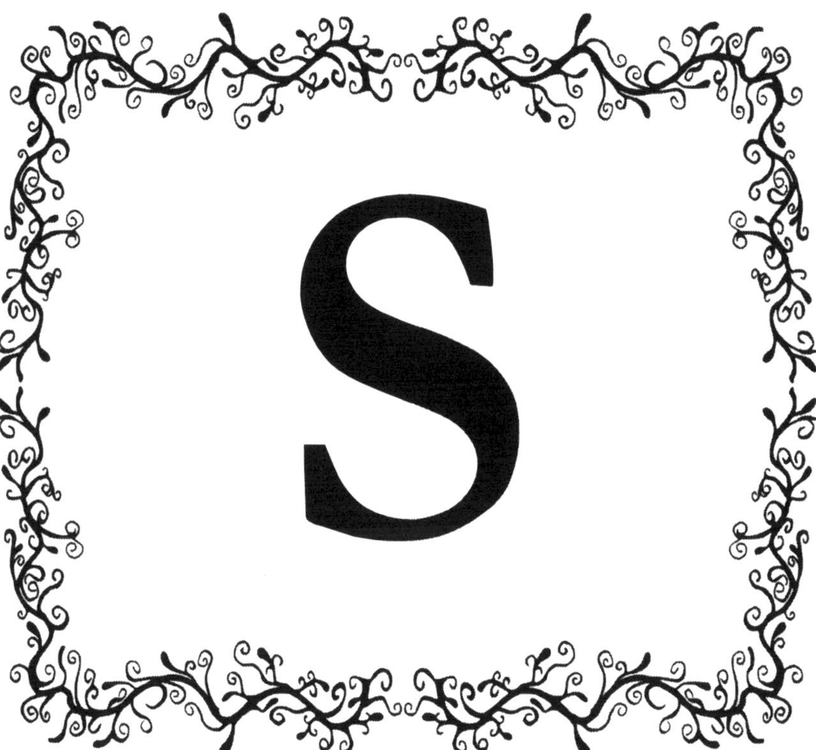
S

My Nana is…

S____________________

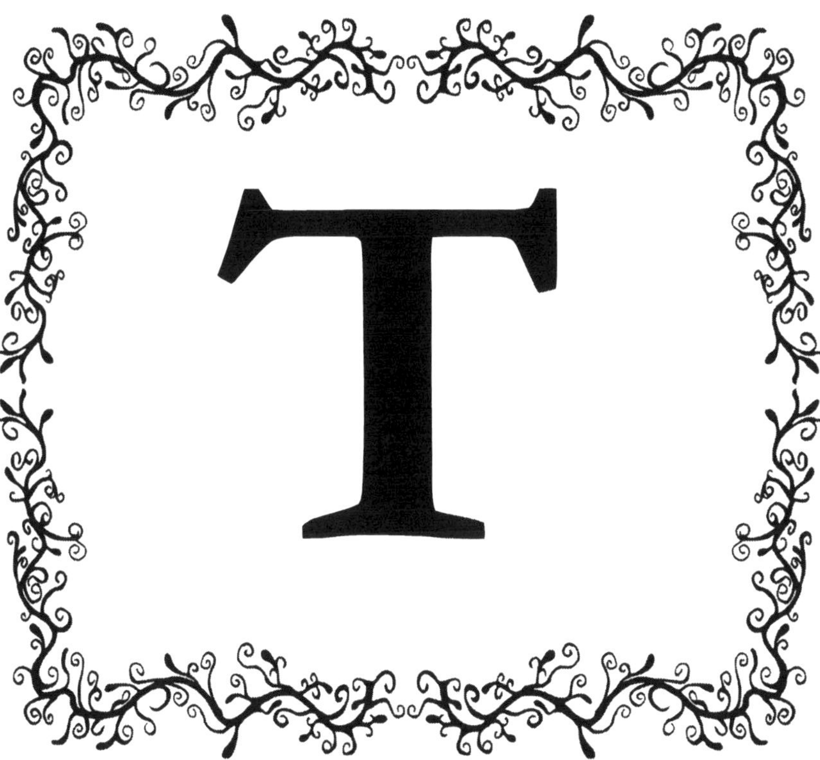
T

My Nana is…

T__________

U

My Nana is…

U__________

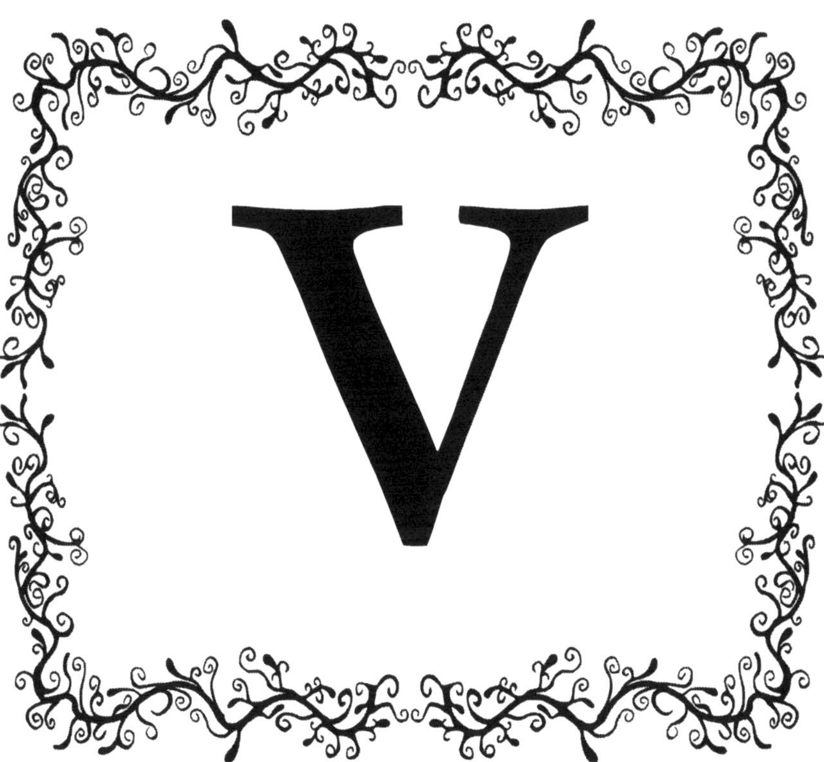
V

My Nana is…

V___________

W

My Nana is…

W________

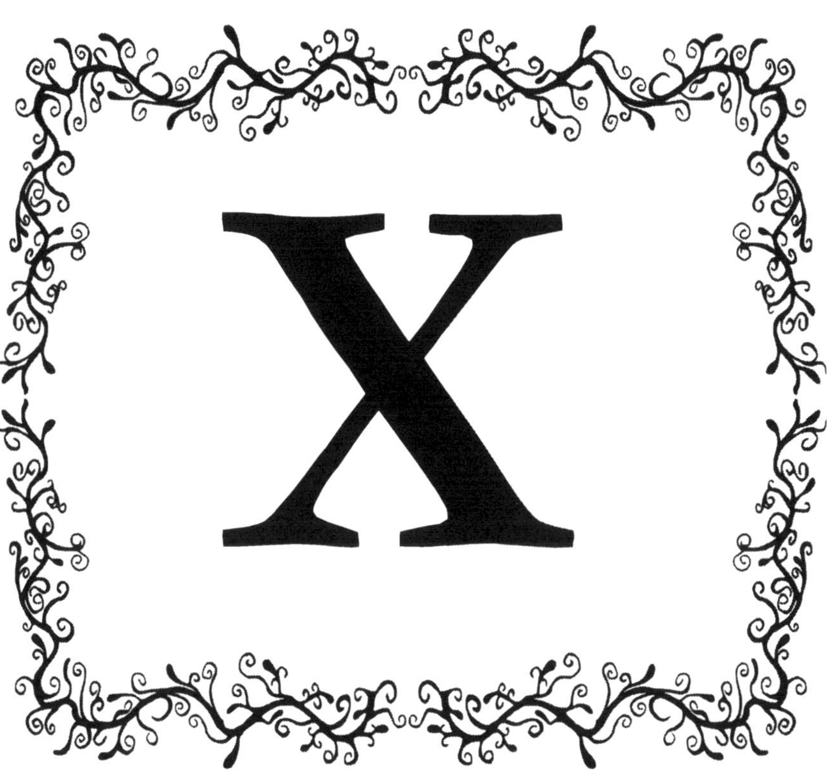
X

My Nana is…

X________________

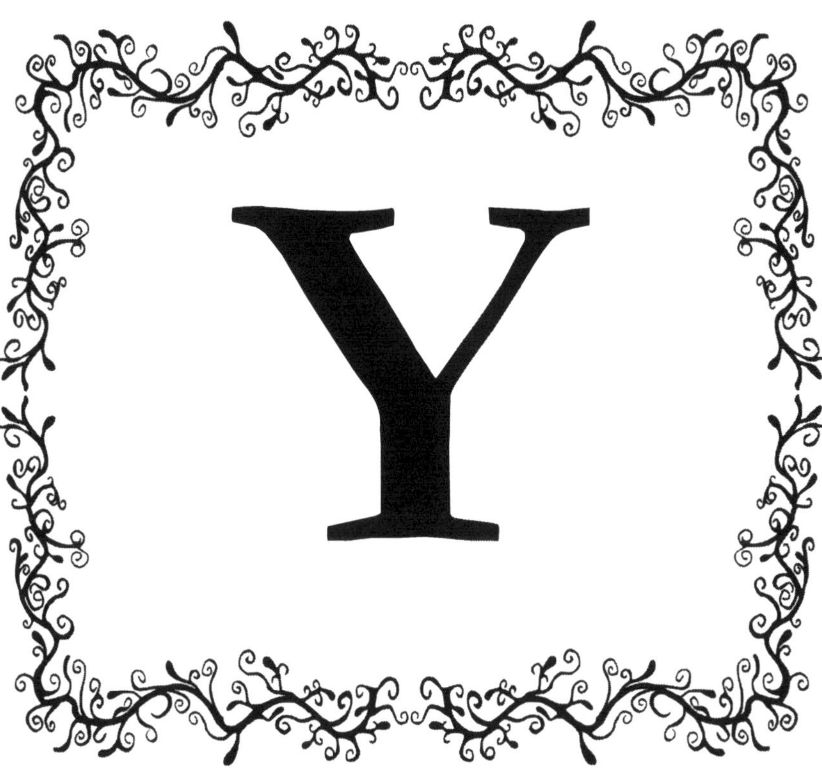
Y

My Nana is…

Y_______________

Z

My Nana is…

Z_______________

Thank You!

Also In This Series

My Dad/Papa A to Z
My Mom/Mum/Mama A to Z
My Son A to Z
My Daughter A to Z
My Husband A to Z
My Wife A to Z
My Sister A to Z
My Brother A to Z
My Uncle A to Z
My Aunt/Auntie/Aunty A to Z
My Grandpa/Grandad/Gramps A to Z
My Grandma/Granny/Nana/Gran/Nanny/Nan A to Z
My Best Friend/Bestie A to Z
My Girlfriend A to Z
My Boyfriend A to Z
My Partner A to Z

29570565R00036

Made in the USA
Middletown, DE
24 February 2016

The Eagle, A Symbol of Freedom

by Tiffany Gibson

PEARSON

Glenview, Illinois • Boston, Massachusetts
Chandler Arizona • Upper Saddle River, New Jersey

Symbols

Symbols are all around you. Symbols are pictures or signs that mean something. A red sign means stop. A heart means love.

The United States has a flag. A flag is a symbol. The United States has other symbols.

The bald eagle is a symbol. It stands for, or means, freedom. Freedom means you can make your own decisions.

13 colonies

Early America

In 1782, there were 13 colonies in America. At first, England made the laws, or rules. The colonies wanted freedom to make their own laws.

Leaders of the 13 colonies

Leaders from each colony had a meeting. They made a new country—the United States. The leaders wanted a national symbol. They wanted the symbol to mean freedom.

The leaders wanted an animal for the symbol. They picked the bald eagle.

To Americans, the bald eagle stands for freedom. The bald eagle is the national symbol of the United States.

Leaders use a stamp with the bald eagle.

Develop Language **Past Tense Verbs**

We add *-ed* to words to show they happened in the past.

Present Tense	Ending	Past Tense
want	-ed	wanted

Franklin wanted a turkey for America's symbol.

A National Turkey?

Benjamin Franklin was a leader in the 13 colonies. He wanted a turkey for the national symbol. He thought turkeys were brave. He thought eagles were lazy.

Today the bald eagle is still a symbol of freedom. A picture of the bald eagle is on a one-dollar bill.

Where can you see America's symbol for freedom?